OBLIQUE PRAYERS

Books by Denise Levertov

Poetry

The Double Image

Here and Now

Overland to the Islands

With Eyes at the Back of Our Heads

The Jacob's Ladder

O Taste and See

The Sorrow Dance

Relearning the Alphabet

To Stay Alive

Footprints

The Freeing of the Dust

Life in the Forest

Collected Earlier Poems 1940–1960

Candles in Babylon

Poems 1960–1967

Oblique Prayers

Prose

The Poet in the World

Light Up the Cave

Translations

Guillevic/Selected Poems

Denise Levertov

Oblique Prayers

New Poems with 14 Translations from Jean Joubert

A New Directions Book

Grateful acknowledgment is made to the editors and publishers of books and magazines in which some of the poems in this collection previously appeared: *And Not Surrender: American Poets on Lebanon* (Arab-American Cultural Foundation), *American Poetry Review, The Amherst Review, The Amicus Journal, Brandeis Essays in Literature* (Brandeis University), *Brandeis Review, Comradery, Hanging Loose, Harvard Magazine, On Equal Terms* (Symposium Press, The University of Alabama), *Pearl* (Denmark), *Ploughshares, Poetry East, Sequoia, Watershed.*

The following poems were originally published as broadsides: "Of Necessity" (Art and Humanities Council of Tulsa), "Mappemonde" (Folger Shakespeare Library), "The Task" (Red Star Black Rose Press, Oakland, Cal.).

The French texts of poems by Jean Joubert are taken from *Les poèmes, 1955–1975* and *Cinquante toiles pour une espace blanc* and published by permission of Société des Éditions Grasset et Fasquelle, © Éditions Grasset et Fasquelle, 1977, 1982.

Manufactured in the United States of America
First published clothbound and as New Directions Paperbook 578 in 1984
Published simultaneously in Canada by George J. McLeod, Ltd., Toronto

Library of Congress Cataloging in Publication Data
Levertov, Denise, 1923–
    Oblique prayers.
    (A New Directions Book)
    1. Joubert, Jean, 1928–   —Translations, English.
I. Joubert, Jean, 1928– . II. Title.
PS3562.E8876O24 1984   811'.54   84-1103
ISBN 0-8112-0908-3
ISBN 0-8112-0909-1 (pbk.)

New Directions Books are published for James Laughlin
by New Directions Publishing Corporation,
80 Eighth Avenue, New York 10011

Content

Author's Note

The four sections of this book represent a thematic, not a chronological order. Similarly, the poems within each section are arranged in what has seemed to me the most appropriate sequence, whether or not it was that in which they were composed.

The section of translations from Jean Joubert requires a word of introduction. Joubert was born in 1928 in Châlette-sur-Loing (Loiret), France. He has lived in Languedoc for the last twenty-five years and teaches American literature at the Université Paul Valéry at Montpellier. He has published novels and children's stories as well as poetry, and his collection *Poèmes: 1955–1975* (Grasset, 1975) was awarded the prize of the Académie Mallarmé in 1978. Most of these poems are taken from a later volume, *Cinquante toiles pour un espace blanc* (Grasset, 1982). I hope to present a book-length selection of translations from his work in the future; meanwhile, it is hoped that these poems will serve to introduce him to the American public.

I
DECIPHERINGS

Decipherings

for Guillevic

i

When I lose my center
of gravity
I can't fly:

levitation's
a stone
cast straight as a lark

to fall plumb
and rebound.

ii

Half a wheel's
a rising sun:
without spokes,
an arch:

half a loaf
reveals
the inner wheat:
leavened
transubstantiation.

iii

A child
grows in one's body,
pushes out and
breaks off:

3

                    nerves
denying their
non-existence
twist and pinch
long after:
after that otherness
floats
far,
thistledown engine,

up and
over
horizon's ramparts.

iv

Felt life
grows in one's mind:
each semblance

forms and
reforms cloudy
links with
the next

and the next:
chimes and
gamelan gongs

resound:

pondering,
picking the tesserae,
blue or
perhaps vermilion,

4

what one aches for
is the mosaic music
makes in one's ears

transformed.

Each life spins
                into its own orbit—rain
of meteor showers, sparkle of—
                          some brittle desire, is it?
                          the stab of deep pain?

Not without tearing
                a few fibers,
                        the magnet forces
pull apart. I. He. Being
                is not referential.

I wake: instant recollection—a shadow
                        threatens my son's life.
Others slide their elongations toward his spirit.

My being, unconformable
                    to his perception,
moves on. Awake, I keep waking.

He survives
            and leaves, moving
through the apparition he sees and
                    away from it.

Again waking, I stretch a hand out
to stop the warning clock.
                    Time is another country.

Squinting toward light:
                a tree has filled it
with green diamonds. Or there's the air, bemused:
                        newfallen snow.

Shock waves of a music
                    I don't hear
as you
        don't hear mine.
                        How they beat on the sea-wall!

The Gaze Salutes Lyonel Feininger
While Crossing the New Jersey Wastelands

A certain delicacy in the desolation:
olive-green the polluted
stretches of grass and weeds, the small
meres and sloughs dark with the darkness
of smoked glass,
gray air at intervals slashed with
rust-red uprights,
cranes or derricks;
and at the horizon line,
otherwise indeterminate,
a spidery definition of viaducts and
arched bridges,
pale but clear in silverpoint.

Nonchalant clouds below me
dangle shadows
into the curved river at Saskatoon.

Atlas of frontiers long-redrawn,
gazeteer of obsolete cities—
a jet-vapor garland
                    stretches and stretches to link
your incantations,
and breaks.
Still audible, stiffly revolving,
the globe of the world
creaks out enticements.
Decades pile up like thunderheads.
O Geography!
               On your thick syrops
I float and float,
I glide through your brew
of bitter herbs.

Múmbulla Mountain,
low and round,
hums in green and hums
in tune, down in the Dreamtime.
World, you grow vaster. Our
time cannot
encompass you.

Blue Africa

for Angela Jackson

As they roam over grassland
the elephants cast
a blue river of shadows.
Their ears flap as they listen.

One evening, caught
in icy wind,
the traffic snarling,
I saw for one moment
their fluent stride, and heard
a quiet in Africa,
hum without menace.
They listened to sunlight,
and flowed
onward, unhurried.
                    Remember,
they are there
                now.
Each in turn
enters the river of blue.

They make mistakes:
they busy themselves,
anxious to see more, straining their necks to look
beyond blue trees at dusk,
forgetting it is
the dust at their feet reveals
the strangest, most needful truth.

They think they want
a cherishing love to protect them
from the anguish they must distribute, the way
       wives of cruel kings handed
       loaves of bread to the poor—
a love that delights in them: but when

ironic Time gives them such love
they discover—and only then—its weight, which,
if they received and kept it, would crush down
the power entrusted to them.
The tender lover,
aghast at what he sees them seeing, or blind
and gently denying it, would set
a wall of lead about them,
hold down their feathered
Hermes-feet,
close the eyes that brim
not with tears but with visions,
silence the savage music
such golden mouths
              are sworn to utter.

With one I learned
how roots turn
to grip loam,
learned
the pulse of stone,
mineral arteries,
skyless auroras.

Was it so indeed?
I remember now
only telling myself
it was so.

Another led me
under the wing of
the waterfall. Light
was fine mist.
My skin was myself.

I remember now
only the words,
what they tell is gone.

And others I loved—
what were their kingdoms?
What songs did I sing of them,
and gazed from what high windows
toward their borders?

I journeyed
onward, my road always
drawing me further.

'But that other:
he danced like a gypsy's bear at the winter crossroads,
the days of your youth and his are a bit of blue glass
bevelled by oceans and kept in his pocket,
wherever he is is always
now.
Touch, mass, weight, warmth:
a language you found you knew.
He brought you
the bread of sunlight on great platters of laughter."

I thought I was growing wings—
it was a cocoon.

I thought, now is the time to step
into the fire—
it was deep water.

Eschatology is a word I learned
as a child: the study of Last Things;

facing my mirror—no longer young,
    the news—always of death,
      the dogs—rising from sleep and clamoring
        and howling, howling,

nevertheless
I see for a moment
that's not it: it is
the First Things.

Word after word
floats through the glass.
Toward me.

Man Wearing Bird

I could be stone,
a live bird on my civic head.
They would not look twice.

This is my pigeon
and I its prophet.
No one but I

found it. It died
for me to find,
to lift like the Host

and place aloft, a soft
weight on my naked scalp,
where one more time

flailing wings can
contest with the wind.
I am a column, a pillar of

righteousness, upholding
mystery, a dead pigeon that spoke
and continues to speak, that told

no one but me what to do,
told me to hold still under its
cold flutterings, told me

to relish the foolish grins, the awestruck
staring of passing, passing,
tenuous motorists, stand

barelegged in the winter day, display—
with the same wind beating
upon it—the number life and its warders

assign me, inscribed on my thin shirt
over my heart:

I the prophet,
chosen from all, ennobled, singular,
by this unique
unfathomable death.

Instead of arms to hold you
I want longer limbs, vines,
to wrap you twofold, threefold.

I wrap you, I pick you up, I carry you,
your knees drawn up, your head bent,
your arms crossed on your breast.

You are heavy.
I walk, I walk.
You say nothing.

Onward. Hill and dale. Indoors.
Out again. You say nothing.
You grow smaller, I wrap you fourfold.

I show you all the wonders you showed me,
infinitesimal and immense.
You grow smaller, smaller,
and always heavier. Why will you not speak?

Fogbillows crest over ocean, soundless, unbreaking,
infinitely patient.

Tier after tier, mountains rehearse
the passage from green to evening's amethyst.

Redwings repeat with unslaked thirst
their one sweet song.

The rain's cleared off and the cats are dreamily
watching the lucid world, perched on the fence-rail,
striving for nothing; their shadows grow long.

Delicately,
two hilltop deer
nibble the sky.

Mexico City—smog and light but no color.
Los Angeles—light and smog but no color.
San Francisco—arid pastels.
Brownstone and grime-gray and black glass—New York.
Boston—trees and clouds but no color.
Tawny Rome!
                    The pearl-gray sheen of Paris.
The dear soot-darkened Portland stone of London.
Soot-darkened stone of London.
Stone of London.
Dear. Soot-darkened. Stone.
Of London . . .

Running before the storm, the older child
was beautiful, her gold hair flew about her,
her small plump legs twinkled amusingly.
It was the other needed help—
wailing, toiling along, a wisp
of misery. Sticky with jam,
her skin damp, her hands
spiders in my hair.
But carrying her, strangely I began
to cherish that discomfort.
The wind blew, the first large raindrops
were falling, the forest we were leaving
leaned darkly after us, waving
in threat or longing.
Quieted, my burden
held fast to me,
patiently trustful. Of necessity.

Grey Sweaters

for James Laughlin

You want your old grey sweater,
lost or given away, you
need it for life and death, your lines
are cast to pull it
back around you.
Last night I dreamed one—
a sweater, I mean, found in the woods,
knit by an oriole.
Once I had—have you seen one ever?
—an oriole's nest,
woven of silvery milkweed silk
and weathered light as a
spindrift timber
tempered ten saltwater seasons . . .
I wore it, a perfect
châtelaine at my waist,
till it slipped off and was lost again
in orchard leaves.
The sweater I dreamed
was like that.
           I meant,
waking, to offer it
as a replacement. It would stretch
to fit you. But then I recalled
that indeed you had conjured yours already
into a poem,
it and your need for it are
the knit and purl of the poem's rows
re-raveled.

Sunlight in Ohio, touching
frostbitten stubblefields
and the cabbagy yards, strewn
       with rusting downhill racers and
       abandoned rabbit-hutches,
of small frame houses near the railroad . . .

The spirit
of Jim Wright is strong here,

so strong it comes through into the train,
through the thick pane.

                The sun's light hands
touch the land
blindly, careful to memorize
planes and expressive
inclinations. It fingers
the scrapyard, the silo'd farm, the schoolbus,
the windowless plant and the men
going in for the dayshift.

             Jim
can't speak anymore, he's dead,
but I swear
he's here
        making me look, he's here
angry and loving and full
of *Sehnsucht*, he's in
this landscape
where industry straggles uncertainly
out into farmland, and farmland
shrinks and looks grey—

he's the kid
skilfully spinning a beat-up bike-wheel
along and along,

down a road that leads straight,
straight, straight to the edge of the world.

One long-dead
   returned for a night
      to speak to us

to me and
   a shadowy other beside me—
      we who had known him in time past—

and to a third,
   our friend, genius of listening,
      fully attentive, smiling.

While the revenant
   spoke, we looked
      back and forth to each other
         across the table,

         wicks taking flame
         one from the next, beacons
         lit on ridges of dark—

         confirming the wonder:

he was telling
   all we had not even
      thought to ask, long ago,

unsuspected luminous eloquence
   of pages long-yellowed,
      interventions

of unrecorded, brick-upon-brick
   structures of early thought
      re-collected,

rooms, towers, arches
   rising from rubble, gateways
      open, inviting entrance:

         dimensions unguessed that change
            a story the way
               our comprehension of some unaccountable flora

         would change
            if we knew a river's course had been altered
               before there were maps—

         altered with effort so strenuous, no-one,
            long after,
               had wanted or tried to remember it.

All we'd thought gone
   into ashes,
      clay,
         deep night—

memories to account for the
   gray unresonant
      gaps and rifts:

his memories,
   which in his life before death had seemed
      obliterate, buried beyond retrieval,

emerging: his gift
   to us, and
      yes, to himself—

visible threads
   woven amongst us, gleaming,
      a fabric
         one with our listening.

II
PRISONERS

O, the great sky!

Green and steep
the solid waves of the land,
breasts, shoulders, haunches,
serene.

The waveless ocean
arches its vertical silver,
molten, translucent.

Fine rain
browses the valley, moves
inland.
And flocks
of sunlight fly
from hill to hill.
The land
smiles in its sleep.

But listen . . .

no crisp susurration of crickets.
One lone frog. One lone
faraway whippoorwill. Absence.
No hum, no whirr.
And look:

the tigerish thistles, bold
yesterday,
curl in sick yellowing.

Drop the wild lettuce!
Try not to breathe!

Laboriously
the spraytruck
has ground its way
this way.
Hear your own steps
in violent silence.

I have been listening, years now,
to last breaths—martyrs dying
passionately
        in open blood,
        in closed cells:

to screams and surprised silence
of children torn from green grass
into the foul bite
           of the great mower.

From a long way off
I listen, I look
with the eyes and ears concealed within me.
Ears and eyes of my body
know as I know:
I have no vocation to join the nameless great,

only to say to others, Watch! Hear them!
Through them alone
we keep our title, *human,*

word like an archway, a bridge, an altar.
(Sworn enemies
answering phrase to phrase,
used to sing in the same key, imagine!—
used to pick up the furious song and
sing it through
to the tonic resting place, the chord,
however harsh,
of resolution.)

Nowadays
I begin to hear a new sound:

a leaf seems as it slowly
twirls down
earthward
to hum,

a candle, silently
melting beneath its flame,
seems to implore
attention, that it not burn its life
unseen.

Thinking about El Salvador

Because every day they chop heads off
I'm silent.
In each person's head they chopped off
was a tongue,
for each tongue they silence
a word in my mouth
unsays itself.

From each person's head two eyes
looked at the world;
for each gaze they cut
a line of seeing unwords itself.

Because every day they chop heads off
no force
flows into language,
thoughts
think themselves worthless.

No blade of *machete*
threatens my neck,
but its muscles
cringe and tighten,
my voice
hides in its throat-cave
ashamed to sound
            into that silence,
the silence

of raped women,
of priests and peasants,
teachers and children,

of all whose heads every day
float down the river
and rot
and sink,
not Orpheus heads
still singing, bound for the sea,
but mute.

The title originally included the date 1982, but alas, the death squads
and the army continue the slaughter, with U.S. help.—D.L., 1984

Perhaps No Poem But All I Can Say
And I Cannot Be Silent

As a devout Christian, my father
took delight and pride in being
(like Christ and the Apostles)
a Jew.
      It was
      Hasidic lore, his heritage,
      he drew on to know
      the Holy Spirit as Shekinah.

My Gentile mother, Welsh through and through,
and like my father sustained
by deep faith, cherished
all her long life the words
of Israel Zangwill, who told her,
'You have a Jewish soul.'

I their daughter ('flesh of their flesh,
            bone of their bone')
writing, in this Age of Terror, a libretto
about El Salvador, the suffering,
         the martyrs,

look from my page to watch
the apportioned news—those foul
dollops of History
each day thrusts at us, pushing them
into our gullets—
         and see that,
         in Lebanon
      so-called Jews have permitted
      so-called Christians
      to wreak pogrom ('thunder of devastation')
      on helpless folk (of a tribe
      anciently kin to their own, and now

concentrated
                    in Camps . . .)

My father—my mother—
I have longed for you.
Now I see
            it is well you are dead,
dead and
gone from Time,
gone from this time whose weight
of shame your bones, weary already
from your own days and years of
tragic History,
could surely not have borne.

In dark slick as
                    plastic garbage bags,
spotlights play, color of
                    canned grapefruit juice . . .
Half-heroes totter
                    into the glare:
America,
         stalking its meat,
                         pounces.

Each time
         the same meal, monotony
of lead-tasting blood.
Catharsis blocked, America
chokes on its own
                    clotted tears.
It is millions,
             each a loner.
                         Meanwhile,
bellies keep swelling,
             limbs dwindle
to bone, famine
             drags its feet over continents.

                    And meanwhile,
screened from half-heroes' ritual mourners
             by smoke of their little fires,
             their beguiled attention fixed
             on dead phantasmal presidents,
             innocuous dead singers,
and unheard while they wail, 'give peace a chance,'

vaster catastrophes
are planned.

As if they had tamed the wholesome undomesticated
        puffball,
men self-deceived are busily cultivating,
in nuclear mushroom sheds, amanita buttons,
embryonic gills undisclosed—rank buds of death.
Men shield their minds from horror, shield their hands
with rubber, work behind glass partitions,
yet breathe in, breathe out, that dust,
spreading throughout themselves, throughout the world,
spores of the Destroying Angel.

Watching *Dark Circle*

'Why, this is hell, nor am I out of it'
Marlowe, Dr. Faustus

Men are willing to observe
the writhing, the bubbling flesh and
swift but protracted charring of bone
while the subject pigs, placed in cages designed for this,
don't pass out but continue to scream as they turn to cinder.
The Pentagon wants to know
something a child could tell it:
it hurts to burn, and even a match
can make you scream, pigs or people,
even the smallest common flame can kill you.
This plutonic calefaction is redundant.

Men are willing
to call the roasting of live pigs
a simulation of certain conditions. It is
not a simulation. The pigs (with their high-rated
    intelligence,
their uncanny precognition of disaster) are real,
their agony real agony, the smell
is not archetypal breakfast nor ancient feasting
but a foul miasma irremovable from the nostrils,
and the simulation of hell these men
have carefully set up
is hell itself,
            and they in it, dead in their lives,
and what can redeem them? What can redeem them?

Gathered at the River

For Beatrice Hawley and John Jagel

As if the trees were not indifferent . . .

A breeze flutters the candles but the trees give off
a sense of listening, of hush.

The dust of August on their leaves.
But it grows dark. Their dark green
is something known about, not seen.

But summer twilight takes away
only color, not form. The tree-forms,
massive trunks and the great domed heads,
leaning in towards us, are visible,

a half-circle of attention.

They listen because the war
we speak of, the human war with ourselves,

the war against earth,
against nature,
is a war against them.

The words are spoken
of those who survived a while,
living shadowgraphs, eyes fixed forever
on witnessed horror,
who survived to give
testimony, that no-one
may plead ignorance.
Contra naturam. The trees,
the trees are not indifferent.

We intone together, *Never again,*

we stand in a circle,
singing, speaking, making vows,

remembering the dead
of Hiroshima,
of Nagasaki.

We are holding candles: we kneel to set them
afloat on the dark river
as they do
there in Hiroshima. We are invoking

saints and prophets,
heroes and heroines of justice and peace,
to be with us, to help us
stop the torment of our evil dreams . . .

Windthreatened flames bob on the current . . .

They don't get far from shore. But none capsizes
even in the swell of a boat's wake.

The waxy paper cups sheltering them
catch fire. But still the candles
sail their gold downstream.

And still the trees ponder our strange doings, as if
well aware that if we fail,
we fail also for them:
if our resolves and prayers are weak and fail

there will be nothing left of their slow and innocent
    wisdom,

no roots,
no bole nor branch,

no memory
of shade,
of leaf,

no pollen.

Though the road turn at last
to death's ordinary door,
and we knock there, ready
to enter and it opens
easily for us,
              yet
all the long journey
we shall have gone in chains,
fed on knowledge-apples
acrid and riddled with grubs.

We taste other food that life,
like a charitable farm-girl,
holds out to us as we pass—
but our mouths are puckered,
a taint of ash on the tongue.

It's not joy that we've lost—
wildfire, it flares
in dark or shine as it will.
What's gone
is common happiness,
plain bread we could eat
with the old apple of knowledge.

That old one—it griped us sometimes,
but it was firm, tart,
sometimes delectable . . .

The ashen apple of these days
grew from poisoned soil. We are prisoners
and must eat
our ration. All the long road
in chains, even if, after all,
we come to
death's ordinary door, with time
smiling its ordinary
long-ago smile.

43

The Cry

Dedicated to Jonathan Schell

No pulsations
        of passionate rhetoric
                suffice
in this time
        in this time
              this time
we stammer in
        stammering dread
                or
parched, utter
        silence
           from
mouths gaping to
        'Aayy!'—
           this time when
in dense fog
        groping
           groping or simply standing
by mere luck balanced
        still
           on the
swaying
        aerial catwalk of
           survival
we've approached
        the last
           the last choice:
shall we
        we and our kindred
           we and
the sibling lives,
        animal,
           vegetable,

we've lorded it over,
                    the powers we've
                              taken in thrall,
waters,
        earths,
                airs,
shall they
        shall we
                by our own hand
undo our
        being,
                their being,
erase
      is
        and *was*
along with
        will be?
                    Nothing
for eloquence
            no rhetoric
                        fits
that *unrendering*,
                voiding,
                        dis-
assemblement—If
                by luck
                        chance
grace perhaps
            able
                    even now
to turn
        to turn away from
                        that dis-
solution—
        only, O
                maybe
some wholly
            holy
                holy

45

unmerited call:
           bellbird
                in branch of
snowrose
      blossoming
            newborn cry
demanding
      with cherubim
            and seraphim
eternity:
      being:
        milk:

III
Fourteen Poems by Jean Joubert

Écriture du vent

à Serge Brindeau

Le poème ici né du matin, de la clarté
liquide où nage encore un songe,
tu le crois grand, tu flaires l'immortel
et te réjouis de ce parfum.
Rose céleste, mauve profond, musique,
tu le vois sûr au centre de la roue
dont tourne et geint dans les brouillards
le fer boueux. Le jour pourtant s'avance,
le poids du sang. Les mots sont vulnérables:
la pluie, le feu, la main qui erre,
l'égarement peuvent les assaillir.
C'est le signe de nos frontières,
il nous défend de l'excessif orgueil.
Il n'y a plus alors que des éclats de langue,
des lettres chues, des loques grises,
comme des voix au loin dans la vallée
que les échos déchirent. Et parfois rien:
le sable, le silence, l'écriture du vent.

Cette autre encore

Cette autre encore,
    terrible femme qui criait sur les collines, pleurant
        la mort d'un roi.
On l'entendait avec effroi du côté des rivières, là
        où s'élèvent les demeures,
où sur le sommeil des jardins tirés à la corde, à la
        houe, le soir penche sa voile rose.

Wind Script

To Serge Brindeau

The poem newborn of morning,
of the liquid clarity where a dream still swims:
you think it great, you catch the scent of immortality
and luxuriate in that perfume.
Celestial rose, profound mauve, music—
you see it securely at the center
of the turning wheel whose muddy iron
creaks through the fog. But the day proceeds,
the weight of blood. Words are vulnerable:
rain, fire, the errant hand,
confusion—all can assail them.
This marks our limits, guards us
from an excess of pride.
Then there are left only splinters of language,
fallen letters, gray tatters
like voices far across the valley,
which echoes fracture. And sometimes nothing:
sand, silence, calligraphy of the wind.

Again That Other

Again that other, the terrible one,
the woman who wailed on the hilltops
lamenting the deaths of kings . . .
With dread her voice has been heard
    by the riverbanks, down among dwellings, where
    over sleepy gardens laid out in rows well tilled,
    the evening reefs-in its rose-colored sail.

L'eau droite y court entre les simples, la terre est
    un berceau de feuilles, tout y prospère dans
    l'oubli des dieux.
Alors pourquoi suivre cette démente, guetter sa langue
    son drapeau?
Certains complotent son massacre, d'autres un rire ou
    un crachat.
Bouche étroite, basse saison! Nos enfants choisiront
    dans la douleur et le mépris.

L'été se clôt

Le
temps
qui nous prendra

nous le
prenons parfois
par la
queue

comme un beau lézard
bleu qui se
brise

Pour un instant
scintille entre nos doigts
la frénétique lueur

There the water
runs a straight course between herbs,
the earth is a leafy cradle,
all prospers there,
forgotten by the gods.
Why then follow this raving woman,
why pay heed to that flag of warning, her tongue?
Some people plot to kill her,
others just laugh and spit.
Narrow mouths,
mean and debased times!
It's our children
who'll have to make choices,
in pain and contempt.

from **L'été se clôt**

Time
which will
take us

we take
sometimes
by the tail

like a handsome blue
lizard which deftly
breaks itself off

For one wild moment
it gleams
between our fingers

Haut lieu de songe de
merveille

(Ainsi de toi Amour et du poème)

Eau de lune

L'œil aiguisé
par ton
visage

j'ai vu au soir
la mer
violette

l'appel des
feux

puis l'eau
de
lune

Venise décembre

Renversée sous la mer, une forêt soutient
    la ville pourrissante,
qui fut lieu de péage, d'épice, de navire,

52

high crest
of dream
of marvel

(Thus it is
with you, Love,
and with the poem).

Moonwater

With eyes made keen
by watching your face

I've seen at dusk
the sea
        violet

the beckoning
    points of light

then:
        moonwater.

December Venice

Up-ended under the sea, a forest supports the decaying
        city
which once was a place of levies, of spices, of a great
        fleet,

53

d'or sombre décharné d'un haut visage:
lieu de génie, de guerre, de sauvages prisons.

Les arbres froids vêtus de sel et dans le noir
portent l'immonde, la merveille.

La ville glisse vers sa mort. Sur ses places
les oiseaux gris cherchent l'ancien
feuillage.

Les quatre réveils

La sourde est morte par une nuit de vent.
Le village sifflait. Des feuilles, des rafales.
Elle tourne dans son silence. L'ampoule nue
faiblit. Aux murs, des ombres louches.
"Je suis en plan," dit-elle, gémit dans le désert
et capitule. A l'aube, elle était froide.
Longtemps vigie à sa fenêtre,
pleureuse noire, rusée sorcière,
son livre d'heures s'est fermé.
Demeurent sur la table
quatre marrons dans une porcelaine,
une serviette grise parmi les miettes
et sur la maie, semblables, côte à côte,
quatre réveils qui continuent de battre.

La sentence

"Vous êtes tous condamnés à mort, dit-il.
La sentence sera exécutée pour chacun d'entre vous

of a lean and haughty countenance cast in somber gold:
place of genius, of war, of savage prisons.

The chill trees robed in salt and blackness
    uphold the squalor, the marvel.

The city is sliding toward its death. In its piazzas
    gray birds look for the long-ago leaves.

The Four Alarm Clocks

The deaf woman died on a windy night.
The village wailed and whistled. Leaves, gusts and
    squalls.
She turns within her silence. The naked bulb
has grown dim. On the walls, enigmatic shadows.
'I'm through,' she said, trembling in the wilderness
and capitulated. By dawn she was cold.
She who for so long kept watch on everyone from her
    window,
black funeral-wailer, wily sorceress—
her book of hours is shut.
On the table remain
four chestnuts in a china bowl,
a gray cloth among crumbs,
and on the dresser, side by side, exactly alike,
four alarm clocks, still ticking away.

The Sentence

'All of you are condemned to death,' he said.
'The sentence will be carried out for each of you

quand et comme il conviendra.
Il n'y a pas d'appel. Rentrez dans vos prisons,
nous saurons vous trouver.
Nous avons le bras long, l'œil aigu, des registres.
En attendant, voici du tabac, de l'alcool.
Jouez, rêvez! Il n'est pas interdit d'imaginer parfois
le goût du dernier verre, de la dernière cigarette."

Chat vieux

Chat vieux comme le
village où je suis
et les racines,

chaque matin tes yeux
(l'un voilé)
sont plus grands.

Que vois-tu dans la brume
entre roche et cyprès? Tu veilles
maintenant couché sur ma poitrine.

Tu te plais à mon sang,
tes griffes me
devinent.

Sur ton échine maigre
je pose cette main
qui sait et ne veut pas savoir.

when and in whatever way it is convenient.
There is no appeal. Return to your prisons,
we shall know how to find you.
We have long arms, sharp eyes, registers.
Meanwhile, here's tobacco and booze.
Go ahead, play, dream! It's not forbidden
to imagine the taste of the last glass sometimes,
or the last cigarette.'

Ancient Cat

Cat
old as this village
old as roots

each morning your eyes
(one of them veiled)
are larger.

What do you see in the haze
between rock and
cypress?
      These days you lie
stretched on my chest
to maintain your vigil.

My blood
pleases you, your claws
read me.

On your scrawny spine I place
this hand
      which knows and
wants not to know.

Le feu craque dans la cuisine, et de grandes vapeurs échevelées collent aux vitres leurs visages.

Sur la table, l'enfant écrit. Penché, le père guide la main qui tremble. "Applique-toi!" dit-il "C'est mieux, c'est bien" puis "Il est tard."

L'enfant écrit *enfant*, et de ce mot s'étonne sur la page, comme d'une bête douce que tantôt, l'encre étant sèche, il pourra du doigt caresser.

De sa plus belle main, le père écrit *miroir* avec des pleins et des déliés, élégamment bouclés entre les lignes (Commis aux écritures à la fabrique).

Miroir copie l'enfant, puis soupire: "J'ai bien sommeil!" "Il neige" dit le père.

L'enfant écrit *Il neige* et, dans son tablier noir bordé de rouge, paisiblement s'endort.

Portrait d'homme

(Holbein)

Moi,
Marcus Silésius,
poète,
je me suis arraché du monde.
Dans la forêt, au plus noir, j'ai bâti
ma tanière de branches.

In the Kitchen

The fire crackles in the kitchen range, and big disheveled clouds of steam stick their faces up against the window-panes.

At the table, the child is writing. Leaning over him, the father guides his wobbling hand. 'Try!' he says. 'That's better—that's good.' Then, 'It's late.'

The child writes, *Child,* and is amazed at this word there on the page, like a friendly animal that soon, when the ink has dried, he'll be able to stroke with his finger.

In his best copperplate hand, the father writes *mirror,* the curves and uprights elegantly curlicued between the lines (he's a copying-clerk at the factory).

Mirror, the child copies; then sighs, 'I'm so sleepy.' 'It's snowing,' the father says.

The child writes, 'It's snowing,' and, in his black red-bordered pinafore, falls peacefully asleep.

Portrait of a Man

(*after Holbein*)

I,
Marcus Silesius,
poet,
I tore myself out of the world.
In the darkest forest
I wove my lair out of branches.

59

Là-bas, dans leurs palais, longtemps j'ai répété
que je voyais grandir le feu et la famine,
j'ai dénoncé l'orage et l'imminence du charnier.
Qui m'écoutait? Quelques fous, quelques enfants,
une femme qui apprêtait ses linges et ses larmes.
Les autres m'ont haï ou méprisé.
On se détourne ainsi des diseurs de lumière!
Dorénavant j'habite le silence,
je me lève à l'heure du sanglier,
j'attends le cerf au seuil de son royaume.
Je vieillis dans l'orgueil, mes oracles m'étouffent.
Parfois, du haut de la falaise,
je regarde très loin fumer les villes:
braises, cendres, déjà poussière.

Troisième hypothèse sur la mort d'Empédocle

Un peu avant la nuit, une voix s'éleva
dans le verger, l'appelant par son nom.
Il avait soupé seul sous la lampe, serré
le pain, le vin, caressé le silence.
Son chat dormait auprès du feu couvert.
C'est alors que la voix monta parmi les branches,
ne disant que son nom, mais si limpide, si
pressante qu'il ouvrit la porte et s'avança
sous les figuiers, à travers le jardin.
Rien n'y avait changé, si ce n'est que la terre
poreuse s'imbibait de l'unique clarté.
Sur le rivage, des bêtes calmes l'attendaient.
Il entra souriant dans l'ombre de la lune.
Nul jamais plus ne le revit.

Back there in their palaces
how long I had told them, over and over,
what I could see: famine and fire
growing and growing;
I warned them of tempests to come,
of carnage impending.
Who listened? Madmen, a few,
children, a few, a woman
making ready her tears and her bands of linen.
The rest either hated me or misunderstood.
That's how they turn away from those who utter the light!
Since then I inhabit silence,
I rise when the wild boar rises,
I await the stag at the threshold of his kingdom.
I have grown old in my pride,
my oracles choke me.
Sometimes, from high on the cliff,
I watch, far off, the smoke of cities:
embers, cinders, ashes—already dust.

Third Hypothesis on the Death of Empedocles

A little before nightfall, a voice was raised
in the orchard, calling him by his name.
He had supped alone under the lamp, cleared away
the bread and the wine, caressed the silence.
His cat was asleep by the banked fire.
It was then the voice rose up among the branches
uttering only his name, but with such clarity,
so insistently, that he opened his door and
went forward under the figtrees, across the garden.
Nothing had changed there, unless it was
that the porous earth drank-in that singular clearness.
By the waterside calm beasts awaited him.
Smiling, he entered the moon shadow.
No one saw him ever again.

61

Est-ce le vent qui nous gouverne?
Celui-ci, passeur d'étangs,
chargé de songes et de crimes?
Ou celui-là, hautain,
ami des neiges où l'esprit
glisse et nage sur les cimes?
Ou bien encore tel autre:
bouffée de rage, haleine de ténèbre,
métamorphose, au petit jour, de la forêt
où tremble une eau de feuilles?
Dans la naissance du verger, chaque matin je m'interroge.
Je sens vibrer les liens qui me marient
à tant d'étoiles invisibles, à la lune
engloutie, au soleil dont le rire
empourpre la colline. Et la sève partout,
d'arbre en arbre, de fleur en fleur,
et dans les veines du jardin, coule
jusqu'à mes paumes qu'elle irrigue.
Un chien marche dans mes yeux. Le
chat bâille près d'une rose, tandis
qu'au loin des pies froissent les branches.
Et la jeune lumière avive la beauté
d'une toile où veille l'archange. Ensemble
nous prions. En silence nous recevons,
nous acceptons ce souffle immense qui nous lave.

Are we ruled by the wind?—that wind
which ferries over the ponds
a freight of dreams and crimes?
Or the haughty wind, familiar
of snowy peaks where the mind
glides and floats?
Or perhaps some other:
bluster of fury, breath of darkness,
the forest transformed, by daybreak,
to a trembling rain of leaves?
In the newborn orchard each morning
I ponder. And sense the vibration
of bonds that wed me
to the great host of invisible stars,
to the sunken moon,
to the sun whose laughter
flushes the hill with crimson.
And everywhere sap is rising
in tree after tree, and flows
in the very veins of the garden towards me, and bathes
the palms of my hands.
A passing dog
walks through my eyes. The cat
yawns by the roses,
magpies jostle the distant branches.
Early light
burnishes a web's perfection
where the archangel keeps vigil. Together
we pray, in silence
receive, accept
the immense breathing which laves us.

Jamais entre les branches le ciel
n'a brillé d'un tel éclat, comme s'il
tendait vers moi toute sa lumière,
comme s'il essayait de me parler,
de me dire quoi, quel pressant mystère
sur cette bouche transparente?
Ni feuille ni rumeur! C'est dans l'hiver,
dans la vacance froide et le silence
que l'air ainsi soudain se creuse
et resplendit. Ce soir, ailleurs,
un ami est entré dans sa mort,
il sait, il marche seul parmi les arbres,
peut-être pour la dernière fois. Tant
d'amour, tant de combats s'effritent,
s'amenuisent, mais lorsqu'il a levé les yeux,
le ciel soudain s'est revêtu
de la même vertigineuse clarté.

L'arrière-saison du poète

Chaque matin en préparant le thé
je songe à l'ami mort.
Le soleil bas transperce les roseaux,
le chat rôde sur le seuil.

Printemps été automne hiver:
chaque saison apporte ses oiseaux
différents, que je nourris de miettes.

Voici novembre,
le rouge-gorge est au logis de branches.

Brilliant Sky

Never between the branches has the sky
burned with such brilliance, as if
it were offering all of its light to me,
as if it were trying to speak to me,
to say—what? what urgent mystery
strains at that transparent mouth?
No leaf, no rustle . . . It's in winter,
in cold emptiness and silence, that the air
suddenly arches itself like this into infinity,
and glitters.

        This evening, far from here,
a friend is entering his death,
he knows it, he walks
under bare trees alone,
perhaps for the last time. So much love,
so much struggle, spent and worn thin.
But when he looks up, suddenly the sky
is arrayed in this same vertiginous clarity.

The Poet's Late Autumn

Each morning, making tea,
I think of my dead friend.
The low sun slants through the reeds,
the cat prowls at the doorsill.

Spring, summer, autumn, winter:
each season brings
its particular birds, whom I feed with crumbs.

Now it's November, the redbreast
haunts its usual tree.

Je suis seul, je n'écris plus, je remercie
les dieux de ce grand vide de lumière.

Parfois, au-dessus des collines,
un *jet* tire un trait blanc
qu'un vent hautain lentement ébouriffe.

I am alone, I write nothing,
                              I thank
the gods for this great breadth
                         of empty light.

At times, over the hills a jet
leaves a white trail
a lofty wind
              slowly unravels.

IV
OF GOD AND OF THE GODS

Rivers remember
      in the pulse of their springs,
      in curl and slide and onrush
      lakeward and seaward,
a touch
shuddering them forth,
a voice
intoning them into
their ebbing and flood:
      fingertip, breath
      of god or goddess in whom
their fealty rests
rendered by being unceasingly
the pilgrim cònversation of waterflesh.

      That remembrance
      gives them their way
to know, in unknowing flowing,
the God of the gods, whom the gods
themselves have not imagined.

God gave the earth-gods
adamantine ignorance.

They think themselves
the spontaneous shimmering of fact—
brilliant wings with no history
of cramped egg or stifling cocoon.

Therein lies their power.

The tall poplar
so late to leaf I thought, the first year,
it had died, but before I left
        it was rippling a close-wrapped cloak, sewn
        with teardrops of green, each held
        by a single stitch,

reaches now, in its time of advent,
for each day's primal shining.
Above the crouched garden, darkly asleep,
                      swing
seraphs, veiled in their own splendor,
        high in the bare pinnacle.

I sing *tree,* making green
school after school of leaf-fish
flicker between the shade and sunlight
in nets of branch,
urging the students to see, to see—

and one says: *I* like
the *brown* tree. So I look:
she has conjured
one of those scrawny northern cedars,
arbor vitae, dead or alive, one can't tell,
earth-brown, sprouting
bits of dry fern-frond from random twigs,
disregarded;

and this tree, behold,
glows from within;
haloed in visible
invisible gold.

To the Morton Bay Figtree, Australia, a Tree-God

Soul-brother of the majestic beechtree,
thy sculpted buttresses only more sharp-angled,
leaves darker, like the leaves of ilex—

vast tree, named by fools who noticed only
thy small hard fruit, the figlike shape of it,
                              nothing else—
not thy great girth and pallid sturdy bark,
thy alert and faithful retinue of roots,
the benign shade under the rule of thy crown:

Arbor-Emperor, to perceive thy solemn lustre
and not withhold due reverence—
may it not be for this, one might discover,
a lifetime led, after all?—not for
those guilts and expiations the mind's clock ticks over,
but to have sunk before thee in deep obeisance,
spirits rising in weightless joy?

The Avowal

For Carolyn Kizer and John Woodbridge,
Recalling Our Celebration
of the 300th Birthday of George Herbert, 1983

As swimmers dare
to lie face to the sky
and water bears them,
as hawks rest upon air
and air sustains them,
so would I learn to attain
freefall, and float
into Creator Spirit's deep embrace,
knowing no effort earns
that all-surrounding grace.

Mouth, horn, cilia, sun—
multiform, multitude, galaxy, cosmos:
blossom on blossom, fragrance on fragrance, tint upon tint:
and no disdain, no clash
of opposites . . .
               But the god of flowers
sits not among petals but inside the minuscule
bulb of all bulbs, a Buddha, a hen on her eggs,
furled in the cell among cells that insists on growth,
sifted in soil, in bins, in leathery hands of gardeners,
sits and sits in the mustard seed.
And the unknown God of the gods
watches and smiles.

As if God were an old man
always upstairs, sitting about
in sleeveless undershirt, asleep,
arms folded, stomach rumbling,
his breath from open mouth
strident, presaging death . . .

No, God's in the wilderness next door
—that huge tundra room, no walls and a sky roof—
busy at the loom. Among the berry bushes,
rain or shine, that loud clacking and whirring,
irregular but continuous;
God is absorbed in work, and hears
the spacious hum of bees, not the din,
and hears far-off
our screams. Perhaps
listens for prayers in that wild solitude.
And hurries on with the weaving:
till it's done, the great garment woven,
our voices, clear under the familiar
    blocked-out clamor of the task,
can't stop their
            terrible beseeching. God
imagines it sifting through, at last, to music
in the astounded quietness, the loom idle,
the weaver at rest.

St. Peter and the Angel

Delivered out of raw continual pain,
smell of darkness, groans of those others
to whom he was chained—

unchained, and led
past the sleepers,
door after door silently opening—
out!
      And along a long street's
majestic emptiness under the moon:

one hand on the angel's shoulder, one
feeling the air before him,
eyes open but fixed . . .

And not till he saw the angel had left him,
alone and free to resume
the ecstatic, dangerous, wearisome roads of
what he had still to do,
not till then did he recognize
this was no dream. More frightening
than arrest, than being chained to his warders:
he could hear his own footsteps suddenly.
Had the angel's feet
made any sound? He could not recall.
No one had missed him, no one was in pursuit.
He himself must be
the key, now, to the next door,
the next terrors of freedom and joy.

i

Dry wafer,
sour wine.

This day I see

God's in the dust,
not sifted

out from confusion.

ii

Perhaps, I thought,
passing the duckpond,
perhaps—seeing the brilliantly somber water
deranged by lost feathers and bits of
drowning bread—perhaps
these imperfections (the ducklings
practised their diving,
stylized feet vigorously cycling among débris)
are part of perfection,
a pristine nuance? our eyes,
our lives, too close to the canvas,
enmeshed within
the turning dance,
to see it?

iii

In so many Dutch 17th-century paintings
one perceives
a visible quietness, to which the concord

80

of lute and harpsichord contribute,
in which a smiling conversation
reposes:
'calme, luxe,' and—in auburn or mercurial sheen
                    of vessels, autumnal wealth
                    of fur-soft table-carpets,
                    blue snow-gleam of Delft—
'volupté'; but also the clutter
of fruit and herbs, pots, pans, poultry,
strewn on the floor: and isn't
the quiet upon them too, in them and of them,
aren't they wholly at one with the wonder?

iv

Dry wafer,
sour wine:

this day I see

the world, a word
intricately incarnate, offers—
         ravelled, honeycombed, veined, stained—
what hunger craves,

a sorrel grass,
a crust,
water,
salt.

Not the profound *dark*
night of the soul

and not the austere desert
to scorch the heart at noon,
grip the mind
in teeth of ice at evening

but gray,
a place
without clear outlines,

the air
heavy and thick

the soft ground clogging
my feet if I walk,
sucking them downwards
if I stand.

Have you been here?
Is it

a part of human-ness

to enter
no man's land?

I can remember
        (is it asking you
         that
         makes me remember?)
even here

the blesséd light that caressed the world
before I stumbled into
this place of mere
not-darkness.

The Antiphon

*'L'Esprit souffle dans le silence
la où les mots n'ont plus de voix'*
Anon

And then once more
all is eloquent—rain,
raindrops on branches, pavement brick
humbly uneven, twigs of a storm-stripped hedge revealed
shining deep scarlet,
speckled whistler shabby and
unconcerned, anything—all
utters itself, blessedness
soaks the ground and its wintering seeds.

'. . . That Passeth All Understanding'

An awe so quiet
I don't know when it began.

A gratitude
had begun
to sing in me.

Was there
some moment
dividing
song from no song?

When does dewfall begin?

When does night
fold its arms over our hearts
to cherish them?

When is daybreak?

I know this happiness
is provisional:

> the looming presences—
> great suffering, great fear—

> withdraw only
> into peripheral vision:

but ineluctable this shimmering
of wind in the blue leaves:

this flood of stillness
widening the lake of sky:

this need to dance,
this need to kneel:
>   this mystery:

The spirit that walked upon the face of the waters
walks the meadow of long grass;
green shines to silver where the spirit passes.

Wind from the compass points, sun at meridian,
these are forms the spirit enters,
breath, *ruach*, light that is witness and by which we witness.

The grasses numberless, bowing and rising, silently
cry hosanna as the spirit
moves them and moves burnishing

over and again upon mountain pastures
a day of spring, a needle's eye
space and time are passing through like a swathe of silk.